4-22-22

To Leora Bowers

with best wishes
for a speedy recovery
From all of us in The
Wesley S.S. Class

IN GREEN PASTURES

IN GREEN
PASTURES

JANE MERCHANT

ABINGDON PRESS
NASHVILLE
NEW YORK

IN GREEN PASTURES

Copyright © MCMLIX by Abingdon Press

Scripture quotations unless otherwise noted are
from the Revised Standard Version of the Bible
and are copyright 1946 and 1952 by the Division
of Christian Education of the National Council
of the Churches of Christ in the U.S.A.

Poems previously published are copyright 1948 by
Abingdon Press; 1953, 1954, 1955, 1956, 1957,
1958 by the Christian Science Publishing Society;
1956, 1957, 1958 by the Curtis Publishing Co.;
1953, 1954, 1955, 1956, 1957, 1958, 1959 by David
C. Cook Publishing Co.; 1956 by Farm Journal, Inc.;
1957 by The Graded Press; 1957, 1958 by The
Methodist Publishing House; 1951, 1952 by the
Mutual Improvement Assn. of the Church of Jesus
Christ of Latter-Day Saints; 1950 by Pierce & Smith;
1956 by Pierce & Washabaugh; 1956, 1957 by the
Progressive Farmer Co.; 1951, 1956, 1957 by the
Salvation Army, Inc.; 1956 by the Sunday School
Board of the Southern Baptist Convention; 1955,
1956, 1957, 1958 by *These Times*; 1953, 1954 by
the *Washington Star*; 1955 by the Westminster Press.

SET UP, PRINTED, AND BOUND BY THE
PARTHENON PRESS, AT NASHVILLE,
TENNESSEE, UNITED STATES OF AMERICA

PREFACE

The psalm we call the twenty-third is in reality, for most of us, the first—the first one we are taught as children, the first one to which we turn for help in any need, the first, most deeply cherished one of all.

Because the twenty-third is the first psalm to me, as to others, it seemed natural that it should become the theme for this book. In expressing something of what this psalm, which speaks with tender intimacy to, and for, each individual heart, means to me, I hope I have been enabled to express a little of what it means to many other hearts—especially to those hearts which have been warmly responsive to my other books. I pray this book may be of service to them, and to many others who strive to follow faithfully wherever our Shepherd leads, whether through green pastures or dark valleys.

JANE MERCHANT

ACKNOWLEDGMENTS

Many of the poems in this book have appeared previously in periodicals and newspapers. Acknowledgment is here expressed to the following publishers:

To *Adult Bible Class* for "Antipathy," "Dawn," "Even So," "First Christmas After Loss," "Guest," "In His Praise," "Metaphors," "On Expressing Thanks," "Photograph," "Recovery," "So Many Benefits," "Through the Valley," and "Well-ordered Days."

To *Capper's Farmer* for "Suggestion."

To *The Christian Home* for "Not Less Than Stars" and "Pedestrian."

To *The Christian Science Monitor* for "All This Again," "Before Departure," "Between the Lines," "Chanticleer," "Color of Green," "Eight Pigeons," "Essence," "Family View," "Good Return," "Mountain Rain," "Oak Leaf and Acorn," "Renewal," and "Unhungering."

To *The Church School* for "All This Day," "Prayer in Quietness," and "The Shepherd's Visit."

To *Classmate* for "Farmer in Town."

To *The Country Gentleman* for "Synonyms."

To *The Farm Journal* for "Never a Last Good-by."

To *Forward* for "December Song."

To *The Improvement Era* for "A Boy Grown Tall" and "Barren Hill."

To *The New York Times* for "The Lifting Hill."

To the Poetry Society of Tennessee *Book of the Year*, 1957, for "The Real One."

To *The Progressive Farmer* for "Always with Wonder" and "Mother's Rest."

To *Quiet Hour* for "Bright Flowering," "He Restoreth My Soul," and "Mother's Garden."

To *The Saturday Evening Post* for "Another Summer," "Certified," "Each Winter," "Known Room," "Of Certain Words," "Returning Prayer," and "Spring Freeze."

To *Sunday Digest* for "No Hills to Climb" and "Reciprocal."

To *These Times* for "A Woman's Way," "After Failure," "Confidentially," "For All the Glory," and "Of Creeping Things."

To *Upward* for "Patterns of Delight."

To *The War Cry* for "Goodness and Mercy Shall Follow Me," "The Easter Story," and "These Are My Thanks."

To *The Washington Star* for "Familiar Vision," "Independence," "Note to a Friend," and "The Song Beyond."

CONTENTS

III. HE RESTORETH MY SOUL

IV. THROUGH THE VALLEY

V. THOU PREPAREST A TABLE

VI. GOODNESS AND MERCY

I

THE LORD IS MY SHEPHERD

The Lord is my shepherd, I shall not want.—*Ps. 23:1*

THE LORD IS MY SHEPHERD

The Lord of earth and heaven,
Of all things great and small,
He is my faithful shepherd;
I shall not want at all.
I shall not want green pastures
In which my heart may rest
And find, by living waters,
New strength for every test.
I shall not want restoring
When I am spent of soul,
And guidance in the good way,
And gentle, wise control.
I shall not want his presence
And comfort in the stark
Bare stony hours of sorrow
When all is cold and dark.
I shall not want fulfilling
Of all my honest needs,
And days made warm by sharing
Kind words and thoughtful deeds.
I shall not want his goodness
And mercy all my days,
And a house of sure abiding
In which to offer praise.

WE THANK THEE, O SHEPHERD-LORD, for the perfect expression of our hearts' inmost needs in the words of thy shepherd-king. Help us so deeply to believe, so faithfully to obey, that our hearts and lives may joyously confirm the truth of these great words. In his name. AMEN.

When the angels went away from them into heaven, the shepherds said to one another, "Let us go over to Bethlehem and see this thing that has happened, which the Lord has made known to us." And they went with haste, and found Mary and Joseph, and the babe lying in a manger.

—*Luke 2:15-16*

THE SHEPHERD'S VISIT

She watched above the manger where he lay.
The sky was marvelously bright outside,
And she must shield his eyes from any ray
That might disturb him; but they opened wide
When shepherds entered. "We have heard a song
And we have seen a glory; this is he,
The Savior men have waited for so long,
The king the prophets promised us would be."

With grace she answered them. "A shepherd-king
Like David, taking gentle, tender care
As you do, of each tiny helpless thing—
So may he be." They smiled at words so fair;
But she remembered, lulling him to sleep,
Good shepherds give their lives to save
   their sheep.

FORGIVE US, LORD, for our halfhearted giving of a portion of our time, a measure of our service, a little of ourselves. Forgive us our withholdings and begrudgings, our secret grumblings at the cost of following thee. We say thou art our shepherd and we shall not want. Enable us to say thou art our shepherd and thou shall not want all that we have to offer unto thee. In the name of him who gave his life for us. AMEN.

16

He will feed his flock like a shepherd,
  he will gather the lambs in his arms,
he will carry them in his bosom,
  and gently lead those that are with young.

—*Isa. 40:11*

NEW MOTHER

"I will let nothing hurt you,"
She told the child asleep;
And wept because the promise
Was one she could not keep.

"But I will never hurt you,"
She said again; and wept,
Knowing it a promise
No mortal ever kept.

"Life has deep hurts," she whispered,
"Which no one can avert.
God help me teach you strength and love
For conquering any hurt."

THOU KNOWEST, FATHER OF ALL, how much we long to save those whom we love from any hurt. And thou knowest that in our human weakness we ourselves often hurt most the ones whom we love best, by our misunderstanding of their aims and our impatience with their purposes. Teach us, O God, and help us teach those within our care the steadfast love that suffers and is kind, through Christ our Lord. AMEN.

And they went away in the boat to a lonely place by themselves. Now many saw them going, and knew them, and they ran there on foot from all the towns, and got there ahead of them. As he landed he saw a great throng, and he had compassion on them, because they were like sheep without a shepherd; and he began to teach them many things.—*Mark 6:32-34*

HIS TEACHING

When Christ was worn and hungry,
He sought a place of rest
Away from crowding people
Each with some loud request;
But found them waiting for him
And did not turn away—
Why is no record given
Of what he taught that day?

Kindness when one is weary—
Too weary to be kind—
Patience with rash impatience
That strains the soul and mind,
Pure self-forgetting service
In every act and thought—
Whatever words he uttered,
These are the things he taught.

DEAR LORD, sometimes we grow so spent we feel we cannot possibly reply pleasantly to one more inconsiderate request. Help us remember that our Master did, and that he calls us in all things to follow him: to be gentle, no matter how tired we are; to be compassionate, no matter how selfish others seem; and to be responsive to others' needs, no matter how great our own. In his name. AMEN.

For the law was given through Moses; grace and truth came through Jesus Christ.—*John 1:17*

THE LAW AND THE BEATITUDES

When Moses sought a mountain,
The people shrank in dread
From billowing clouds of darkness
Lest they be stricken dead.

When Jesus sought a mountain,
It was a sunlit day,
And multitudes drew near him
And none were warned away.

When Moses left a mountain,
The evils that he saw
Caused him to break, in anger,
The tables of the law.

When Jesus left a mountain,
He saw the motley, mean,
And needy crowds; and straightway
He made a leper clean.

FATHER IN HEAVEN, we thank thee for the law, which is our schoolmaster to lead us to Christ. And we thank thee that to these great revealings of thy will were added the grace and truth of the Sermon on the Mount, and all the gracious words of Christ our Lord. Most of all we thank thee, Father, for Christ's perfect living of the truth he taught. And we beseech thee, in full consciousness of our failures, that we may be enabled to live our lives more nearly in accordance with that truth. In his name. AMEN.

Pray to your Father who is in secret; and your Father who sees in secret will reward you.—*Matt. 6:6*

BRIGHT FLOWERING

Why am I happy, suddenly,
As if good fortune had come to me?

It's not for tidings that I have heard;
It's not for sunlight or singing bird.

The weather's dismal, and my affairs
Are full as ever of irksome cares.

It's all of the thankfulness—out of season—
That I couldn't feel when I had reason.

It's all of the cheer, now real and glad,
That I tried to show when my heart was sad.

All glory to God for prayers that flower
In an unexpected, unlooked-for hour.

WE THANK THEE, OUR FATHER, that thou hearest all our secret prayers to thee for strength and help, and seest all our faltering attempts to live our prayers. We thank thee that thou dost reward us, Lord, for faithfulness in prayer with hours of inward harmony and glad contentment that owe little to external circumstances. May we ever pray with confident expectancy, assured that though we seem to receive no immediate answer to our prayers, the answer will come as certainly and as beautifully as seeds develop into blossoms. In Christ's name. AMEN.

Give to him that asketh thee, and from him that would borrow of thee turn not thou away.—*Matt. 5:42, K.J.V.*

"TURN NOT AWAY"

I may not give to all who ask of me
The thing they ask; a sleekly gleaming knife
Might please a small boy momentarily—
And cause a wound that he would bear for life.
The compromising coins that beggars ask
Might buy a guilty counterfeit of good.
I must refuse them, for the harder task
Of helping them to earn a livelihood—
Must often strive to give some better thing
Than what is asked; to see in all demanding
Requests the hope to which all hearts must cling
For human sympathy and understanding.
I may not give the thing for which they plead—
Nor ever turn away from any need.

OUR HEAVENLY FATHER, who ever givest good things to those who ask thee, give us wisdom in our giving to those who ask of us. Grant that our giving may never be a careless gesture, a means of buying self-esteem at the expense of those to whom we give. May we realize that any human being's appeal to us for gifts and favors, however trifling it may seem, places on us a responsibility that we must not evade. Help us ungrudgingly not only to give outward things, but to "give for alms those things which are within"—our interest, sympathy, and warm solicitude. In Christ's name. AMEN.

The measure you give will be the measure you get.—*Matt.* 7:2

RECIPROCAL

I wanted to say to you,
"Be kind to me today.
My heart is strangely sorrowful;
Be kind in all you say."

Instead I spoke to you
As softly as I could
In warm, commending words
Of gentle things, and good.

And you were kind and pleasant
As anyone could be.
You said, "My heart was deeply sad
Until you spoke to me."

FATHER IN HEAVEN, we thank thee for those times when we have mastered our own feelings of depression enough to speak a cheering word to someone else. We thank thee for the gladness of discovering that we have been enabled to give the help we needed. Help us, Lord, to think of thee and not of ourselves, to think of others' needs and not our own. In Christ's name. AMEN.

Whatever you wish that men would do to you, do so to them; for this is the law and the prophets.—*Matt. 7:12*

EVEN SO

Keep me, Lord, from reasoning thus:
"Since Mary didn't visit us
In our grief, I need not go
To her. Since Clara didn't show
Appreciation of my gift,
I'll send no more. Since Sue can drift
For years and never send a word,
I'll just pretend I haven't heard
About her marriage—though she might
Be pleased, perhaps, if I should write."

Help me, Lord, to pay the call
I wanted to receive, give small
Gifts that I am sure will be
Of help, although I never see
Signs of gratitude, and send
The note I longed for to a friend.

Help me treat folk, not as they
Have treated me, Lord, but the way
That I would have been deeply glad
If they had.

KEEP US, LORD, from measuring ourselves and others by the petty inches of our own self-interest and vanity; help us to measure always by the Golden Rule. In Christ's name. AMEN.

Truly, I say to you, if you have faith as a grain of mustard seed, you will say to this mountain, "Move hence to yonder place," and it will move; and nothing will be impossible to you.

—*Matt. 17:20*

METAPHORS

Faith is a light?
But eyes may be
Too full of tears,
Sometimes, to see.

Faith is an anchor?
But the strain
Of storm may snap
An anchor's chain.

Faith is a seed.
In dark and storm
It grows, unseen,
And safe, and warm.

It will bear harvest
For your need.
Plant deep and well.
Faith is a seed.

HEAVENLY FATHER, grant that our faith in thee may have the vital upward-thrusting force of a living seed, which is not at the mercy of darkness or of storm, but which grows and flourishes in spite of them. Grant that our faith in thee, O God, may be an active, potent faith, able to move dark mountains of hatred, fear, and selfishness from our own lives and the lives of others. In Christ's name. AMEN.

You shall love your neighbor as yourself.—*Matt.* 22:39

ANTIPATHY

I met one woman, long ago,
For whom I felt, with all dismay,
Such loathing as I did not know
Within my being lay.

Her furtive, darting, evil eyes,
Her poking, prying, clutching fingers—
The horror and the sick surprise
Of that one meeting lingers.

Oh, much would I have sacrificed
To feel some human kindness stir.
I hope, I hope, the loving Christ
Forgives me her.

FORGIVE US, LORD, our reasonless dislikes for other human beings. And if there is reason for our dislike, if we glimpse within another person's heart spitefulness and evil from which we instinctively recoil, forgive us still, O Father of us all, for feeling only revulsion instead of compassion and concern for one who is deeply in need. Give us grace to think, feel, and act in the spirit of Christ, who sought for unpleasant, rejected people and transformed them by the outreach of his understanding love. In his name. AMEN.

Now may the God of peace who brought again from the dead our Lord Jesus, the great shepherd of the sheep, by the blood of the eternal covenant, equip you with everything good that you may do his will, working in you that which is pleasing in his sight, through Jesus Christ; to whom be glory for ever and ever.—*Heb. 13:20-21*

THE EASTER STORY

Lord, I rejoice in all the Easter glory
Of Christ triumphant over death and gloom,
Reading again the old, beloved story
Of grieving women—and an empty tomb,
Of men who walked a lonely road in sadness,
Men rendered desolate by loss and fear,
And how their grief was changed to holy gladness;
These are the stories that I love to hear.

Yet, Lord of love, unless I learn to say
With all my heart, "Forgive them, for they know
Not what they do," when others hurt, betray,
Or mock me, and unless I whisper low,
"Thy will be done," when I must suffer pain—
I know I hear the story all in vain.

FATHER IN HEAVEN, wrongs done to us seem large and difficult to pardon; the pain we feel seems quite unjust and hard to bear. Help us, O God, to measure by the cross, where Christ bore and forgave the cruelest betrayals and the harshest wrongs of men. Help us to cleanse our hearts of every furtive vestige of resentment and rebellion, that we may truly share the resurrection joy. In Christ's name. AMEN.

II

IN GREEN PASTURES

He maketh me to lie down in green pastures: he leadeth me beside the still waters.—*Ps. 23:2, K.J.V.*

IN GREEN PASTURES

Upon green grass,
Beneath green leaves,
By gentle streams
My heart receives
Surcease from strain,
Abiding balm,
Deep amplitudes
Of healing calm.

In scanty quarters,
Dark and bare,
My heart sometimes
Has been aware
Of One who makes
The narrowest space
An ample green
And growing place.

Most GRACIOUS SHEPHERD, who ever leadest us in the way that is best for us, we praise thee for all green and pleasant places where our spirits have found sustenance and rest. We are profoundly, wholly grateful for the sense of thy nearness which we feel amid the quiet beauty of growing things. But above all we are grateful for times of awareness of thy presence that bring a sense of large release and peace to us in little crowded places. In Christ's name. AMEN.

He brought me forth into a broad place.—Ps. 18:19

AFTER A COUNTRY DAY

Now we have satisfied ourselves
That shining mountains keep
Faith with the sky and faith with us;
That fields of wideness sweep
In rich brown furrows, or in rich
Green of exuberant grass
Up to the sunlit mountains' feet;
That myriad wildwoods mass
Their shadowy cool mysteries
Of leaves about the flowing
Of large calm rivers, and little streams
Excited in their going.

Confirming ancient certainties
Is never an idle thing,
And each heart needs to verify
The countryside, in spring.

WE THANK THEE, LORD, for all of springtime's bright renewals in field and hill and wood, and for the joyous privilege of being part of these renewals. We who must spend our usual days in constricted places thank thee for every liberating glimpse of large vistas and uncluttered space. Grant, Lord, that in whatever cramped routines our customary days are spent, our minds may keep wide horizons and our hearts broad sympathies. In Christ's name. AMEN.

OAK LEAF AND ACORN

I've an oak leaf and an acorn
I picked up off the ground
Beside the merry water
Of the little creek you found.

We had come up together
Through the blue mountain air
I'd loved afar, not dreaming
Of ever being there.

The little creek was golden-brown
Save where it rippled whitely
Around the rounded pebbles.
It touched our fingers lightly,

And then we had to leave it;
But let nobody say
An oak leaf and an acorn
Are all I brought away.

WE ARE ABIDINGLY GRATEFUL, OUR FATHER, for all relaxed and happy times of freedom from our ordinary cares, for all high hours of good companionship in lovely places. We praise thee for the special days of shared delight that shine in our remembrance like the sunlit peaks of mountains, giving a warm glow to our dullest lowland days. And we pray thou wilt remember, and help us to remember with compassion all people who have had few, or none, of these glad experiences. In Christ's name. AMEN.

This is rest;
    give rest to the weary;
and this is repose.

—Isa. 28:12

MOTHER'S REST

The doctor said my mother ought to rest
A full hour, after lunch, but when I tried
Reminding her, today, of his behest,
She was too busy poking around outside
To pay attention to me. "Look, I found
A violet," she said. "There'll soon be more.
The jonquils are away out of the ground;
There'll be a bloom next week, if not before.
And see, the jasmine is about to flower—
Lie down and rest? Good land, child, lying flat
Counting wallpaper blossoms for an hour—
There's nothing makes me half as tired as that.
But just to walk on greening earth and see
Small growing things is really rest to me."

For all the healthful rest that weary bodies and tired
minds may find among new unfoldings of leaves and blossoms,
Lord, we offer thanks. For the gladness of rediscovering spring
and being sure once more of the integrity of earth, and seed,
and sun, we praise thee, Lord of all. Of thy good mercy grant,
we pray, that all who have deep need of earth's perennial reassurances may have a green and flowering place of rest and
peace. In Christ's name. amen.

> Awake, O north wind,
>   and come, O south wind!
> Blow upon my garden,
>   let its fragrance be wafted abroad.
>
> —*Song of S. 4:16*

MOTHER'S GARDEN

A stretch of bare red earth when she arrived,
It is a place of sweet surprises now.
A slim young elm and four dogwoods have thrived
In gratitude for love, and they allow
Space for a lilac, and a bridal wreath,
A pussy willow, and a golden bell—
"No proper garden ever yet beneath
The sun lacked those," she says; and she will tell
Us that their blossoms, and the daffodils,
The irises, the sweet peas, and the deep
Red roses whose enchanting fragrance fills
The air, are not, of course, for her to keep.
"Half of the joy of raising them," she'll say,
"Is in the joy of giving them away."

HELP US, DEAR LORD, to learn to share whatever good and lovely things are in our keeping. Help us to learn the grace of patiently planting and cultivating whatever place thou givest us that it may be beautiful and fruitful, not only for ourselves but for the sake of others. May our giving to others of our gifts, our interest, and our time become as natural and spontaneous as the silent opening of the petals of a flower. In Christ's name. AMEN.

But if God so clothes the grass of the field, which today is alive and tomorrow is thrown into the oven, will he not much more clothe you, O men of little faith? —*Matt. 6:30*

SUGGESTION

If you have worry,
If you have woe,
Take it to a meadow
Where green things grow;

Where green things grow
In swift upsurging,
Earth and heaven
In greenness merging.

Watch troubles dwindle—
For worry is one
Thing that will seldom
Thrive in the sun.

Thou knowest, lord, how often we become unduly concerned with ourselves and our own problems and griefs. Thou knowest we need, sometimes, a place where nothing is concerned with anything but growing, where we may for a while forget ourselves and all our cares. Warm our chilly spirits, Father, with the fervent sunshine of thy presence, and clothe them with a green tranquillity of faith and hope. In Christ's name. AMEN.

They shall spring up like grass amid waters,
   like willows by flowing streams.

—*Isa.* 44:4

COLOR OF GREEN

We thought the pines were green
When fields were deep in snow—
But look at the grasses' sheen,
Look where the willows blow
Airily fresh and clean—
This is the color of green!

How strange that we didn't know
The pines are a rusty brown,
How strange that they seemed to glow
Bright green when the snow danced down?
Oh, we were foolish then!—
But pines will be green again.

WE PRAISE THEE, LORD, that thou doest for us exceedingly abundantly above all that we think or ask, in the astonishing vividness of green in spring, in the unexpected blessings that come to us at any time. We praise thee for all the varied shades and hues of green that bring us pleasure, each in its own season; we praise thee, Father, that always there is green, that always there is good. We praise thee in Christ's name. AMEN.

Pleasant words are like a honeycomb,
   sweetness to the soul and health to the body.

—Prov. 16:24

SYNONYMS

I know, of course, uncounted synonyms
For summer: words whose syllables recall
The sleepy, flowering magic that overbrims
The earth with lush repleteness; words that fall
As warmly and as softly on the ear
As sun on cloverbloom, with memories
Of hue and scent so keen we almost hear
In them the elfin thunder of the bees.

Such words are "daisy" and "alfalfa hay,"
"Blackberry" and "Queen Anne's lace";
   but there is one
So reminiscent of ecstatic, gay
Delight in blossoms honeysweet with sun
That to express all summer in a word
I need to utter only "hummingbird."

DEAR LORD, we treasure well all warmly evocative words that bring into our minds bright memories of golden summer days, when all thy creatures, great and small, rejoice in plenteous good. Help us, Father, always to remember the great power there is in words to change a mood for good or ill. Help us to choose our words with faithful care, that they may bring pleasantness and cheer to those who hear. In Christ's name. AMEN.

36

Let them praise the name of the Lord,
　　for his name alone is exalted;
　　his glory is above earth and heaven.

—Ps. 148:13

OF CREEPING THINGS

Because the psalmist, in his litany
Of all who should unite to praise the name
Of the excelling Lord, included wee,
Small creeping things of earth, of little fame,
Along with kings and princes, and the tall
Green wealth of cedars, and gentle beasts that graze
In pleasant pastures—I am sure that small
Voiceless existences are also praise.

Even the tiniest glowworms praise him well
With bright illuminations of his laws;
The mollusk glorifies him with its shell,
And spiders honor him with airy gauze,
And faithfully as fruitful trees, or hoary
Upsurging mountain heights, declare his glory.

WE PRAISE THEE, O GOD, who hast created all things for thy glory. Sun and moon and stars, and fire and hail and snow and stormy winds, and all diversities of living things, praise thee by their obedience to thy laws. Grant that as we learn more and more concerning the operation of these laws, we may praise thee more and more, not growing vainglorious because of our knowledge and the power it gives us, but reverently awed before thy glory and thy power. In the name of Christ. AMEN.

For affliction does not come from the dust,
    nor does trouble sprout from the ground;
but man is born to trouble
    as the sparks fly upward.

—*Job* 5:6-7

SEASON OF GRASS

The child in us all has lain
Face buried in grass—earth cool
And soft yet firm beneath the yielding grass.

Our tears never singed the grass or
    scorched the earth.
Our bodies shook with sobs but earth did not,
And slowly our fevered eyes grew cool again.

Now, breathing cool of grasses on the wind
The child in us all remembers,
And we say to the children of this summertime,

"We cannot spare you grief—we cause you grief.
But may there be for each of you, at least,
Earth steady beneath your sobs,
Grass for your tears."

FATHER IN HEAVEN, who gavest thy Son to be a child, and to feel a child's bewilderment and hurt at grownups' exacting ways, and to grow in comprehension as children often must by pain and struggle, we pray thy compassionate help for all children in their hours of loneliness and grief. Help us to be just and fair and loving in all our dealings with children, so that necessary denials and discipline may leave no unhealing wounds within their hearts. In Christ's name. AMEN.

Provide things honest in the sight of all.—*Rom. 12:17, K.J.V.*

THE REAL ONE

The child was the only early-rising one,
And, slipping out alone before the sun,
She saw the rabbit in the violet border
And held herself as still as dew in order
To see, to see, to see it where it sat.
It was a rabbit, she was sure of that;
It had the lengthy enviable ears
That a rabbit has wherever it appears
On wall or Easter card or handmade quilt.
But this one had an ear that seemed to wilt,
And when it moved to take a larger bite
Of violet leaves, its left hind leg hung light
And didn't move. This rabbit lacked the air
Of the perky rabbits pictured everywhere.
Something about it made her want to try
To hold it close and tell it not to cry.

The grownups came. The real one limped away.
She didn't tell on it. But from that day
She viewed with a reproachful, puzzled look
The beaming rabbits in her storybook.

God of all truth, help us to value truth and honesty too much to give a sentimentally misleading picture of reality to anyone. Save us from fostering for any reason, illusions that may lead to disillusion and cynicism. In Christ's name. AMEN.

39

The floods have lifted up, O Lord,
   the floods have lifted up their voice,
   the floods lift up their roaring.

—Ps. 93:3

FORBEARANCE

They will go back to their drowned homes again
As soon as the spreading waters ebb a little.
They will sweep out the mud and trash and
   scrub the floors
And salvage an iron bedstead and grandma's kettle,
And settle to life once more. They will not complain
Or curse the Lord for sending them too much rain.

They will not go out on the hills and
   plant pine seedlings.
They will not stop emptying trash into the river.
When the waters bring mud and junk into their houses,
They will move out and back, as patient as ever,
And settle to life once more. They will not complain
Or curse the Lord for sending them too much rain.

GRANT THAT WE NEVER impute to thee, O God, the evils that
we bring upon ourselves, by our laziness and greed and lack of
foresight, by our stubborn refusals to work with one another
and with thy laws instead of against them. Save us from passive
acquiescence in evils which we have the power of overcoming;
preserve us from enduring, with an air of martyred resignation,
the havoc and desolation wrought by human folly. Help us,
Lord, in all things, to overcome evil with good. In Christ's name.
AMEN.

40

Faithfulness will spring up from the ground,
and righteousness will look down from the sky.

—Ps. 85:11

THE LIFTING HILL

The hill was a red scar against the sky.
The hill was a red welt upon his heart.
With endless stubborn patience he would try
To fill the gullies and give grass a start
No furious rush of rains could sweep away.
After each gully-washer he was there
To seed the raw and crimson-dripping clay
Again, and yet again; this was his prayer.

Not that the hill was his, or that he had
A soul belonging to him who would view
His work with pride. Some people thought him mad,
And when he died, alone, not many knew.
Not many will recall the man I mean;
But on the lifting hill the grass is green.

WE THANK THEE, OUR FATHER, for all who work with faithful diligence to preserve the usefulness and beauty of the land. Bless and encourage, Lord, all those who labor unselfishly and persistently to save the soil, and all of us whose lives depend upon the soil, from all the evils of hunger, flood, and human degradation that reckless depletion of the earth brings in its wake. May we be always mindful of our responsibility to future generations for right use and conservation of the rich resources thou hast given us. In Christ's name. AMEN.

Break forth into singing, O mountains,
O forest, and every tree in it!

—*Isa.* 44:23

CERTIFIED

No matter what the poplars do
In fervent gold on ardent blue,
No matter how the dogwoods blaze
In frantic crimson to amaze
Our eyes, no matter how the wild
Cherry holds us still, beguiled
By sight of leaves like tawny leather
Whirling through the sunlit weather—
We know it's never really fall
Till the giant maple, last of all,
With red beyond all hope or reason
Consents to certify the season.

OUR HEARTS REJOICE, O FATHER, in the transfiguring radiance of sunlight on the myriad brilliances of autumn leaves. We thank thee for the diverse glories of each tree, which blend with one another in rich harmonies of color. As the infinitely varied hues blend into a unity of loveliness, so may thy people, Lord, keeping their separate individualities, form a united and harmonious whole to serve thee and to praise thee. In Christ's name. AMEN.

The tree of the field is man's life.—*Deut. 20:19, K.J.V.*

FAMILIAR VISION

I do not wish to look at any tree
As if I had not seen a tree before.
I wish to look at it with memory
Of strange years solaced by the trees that soar
Lightly, incredibly into blue air
With such complete and unpretending grace
That they assure my heart, by being there,
I am not friendless in an alien place,
Not uncompanioned in a foreign world,
But deeply kindred to the clean design
Of every leaf undoubtingly unfurled
On any wind. They make this planet mine,
The known trees rooted in familiar loam,
Giving my lonely heart a sense of home.

FATHER IN HEAVEN, in the overwhelming hours when doubts
and dreads assail us, grant us to feel our unity with the in-
domitable persistencies of life thou hast created. Renew our confidence in thee and in the possibilities of the world that thou
hast made, and in our ability, with thy help, to venture courageously, to live creatively, and to grow in grace. Through Christ
our Lord. AMEN.

O come, let us worship and bow down,
  let us kneel before the Lord, our Maker!
For he is our God,
  and we are the people of his pasture,
  and the sheep of his hand.

—*Ps.* 95:6-7

NEEDING THE SOLACE

Forgive me, Lord, if I have loved too well
The ordinary kindnesses of earth,
The known place where my special people dwell
In quietness, the sudden sparkling mirth
Of little showers on dusty summer grasses,
The certainty and unexpectedness
Of every season as it comes and passes,
Bringing old joys for me to repossess.

Needing the solace of a lovely thing
To stir my heart sometimes from heavy grief
I have loved well a redbird's flaming wing,
A jaunty daffodil, a spangled leaf—
And surely the only wrong in this would be
If I had ever loved them more than thee.

ALWAYS WE WOULD THANK THEE, LORD, for thy unfailing
blessings, for all thy merciful and wise and generous care. But
grant, O God, that we may never seek for thy gifts more than
we seek for thee. Grant that our gratitude may go beyond what
thou givest to what thou art; grant us to worship thee, in all
circumstances, with fervently adoring hearts, in spirit and in
truth. Through Christ our Lord. AMEN.

III

HE RESTORETH MY SOUL

He restoreth my soul: he leadeth me in the paths of righteousness for his name's sake.—*Ps. 23:3, K.J.V.*

HE RESTORETH MY SOUL

Almost it seems discourteous, dear Lord,
This turning of my darker side to thee
And showing thee perplexities and griefs
That I permit no human eyes to see,
And offering my brighter side to others
Who seem so much in need of any cheer
That I can give, I hesitate to add
To all their burdens by a single tear.

But I am sure it is not rudeness, Lord.
I long indeed to offer thee my best,
But only thou canst light my spirit's darkness
That there may be a bright side for the rest.
In giving my best to those with whom I dwell
I think I give it, Lord, to thee as well.

FATHER IN HEAVEN, we thank thee that when our souls are cast down and disquieted within us, we still may hope in thee. Always we need thy help, Lord, which no one else can give; our souls become smudged with the clinging soot of trivialities and need thy cleansing; they become worn with the stresses and pressures of living and need thy restoring; they become confused with the many choices that must be made and need thy guidance. Grant that we may never fail to seek the help we need, for our own good and for the good of others. In Christ's name. AMEN.

> Weeping may tarry for the night,
>   but joy comes with the morning.

—Ps. 30:5

DAWN

I have seen the dawn begin
With a thread of lavender
Hinting, to my leafless sight,
There is something more than night.

I have seen the dawn begin
With a sky of scarlet fire
Declaring, high above each tall
Leafy tree, that day is all.

Whether that reviving ray
Shines with great or little power
On barren tree or grassy lawn
Matters little—it is dawn.

WE PRAISE THEE, O GOD, for all restorings of light to our darkness, for the relief and joy that the first faint rays of dawn bring to those who watch and are weary with waiting. We pray thy gracious encouragement, Lord, for all who are wakeful through the hours of darkness, for all who suffer, and for all who weep. Strengthen their spirits and sustain their faith in the coming of dawn, and give them gladness, Lord, through all the day. In Christ's name. AMEN.

When my soul was embittered,
　　when I was pricked in heart,
I was stupid and ignorant,
　　I was like a beast toward thee.
Nevertheless I am continually with thee;
　　thou dost hold my right hand.

—*Ps. 73:21-23*

RETURNING PRAYER

I thank thee, Lord, that thou hast not withdrawn
One tint from diverse radiances of dawn
For lack of thanks from me, hast not diminished
The number of the stars, or left unfinished
One snowflake, flower, or leaf, for want of praise
For these sustaining mercies of my days.

Receive my gratitude, long overdue,
For blessings all the tinted dawns renew,
For faithful friends, for work and rest and mirth,
Splendor of sky and fruitfulness of earth—
And that, when I am thankless, tired and fretful,
Lord, thou art never weary or forgetful.

UNCHANGING LORD, thou knowest our changefulness. Thou knowest the variations of our moods, and that our hearts sometimes are dry and empty of any praise. Thou who art ever blessing us in countless daily ways, renew our spirits to delight in all thy blessings. And grant, O steadfast Father, that even in weariness and sadness, before thy renewing comes, we may steadfastly persevere in striving to do thy will so far as we may know it. In Christ's name. AMEN.

For everything there is a season, and a time for every matter under the heaven.—*Eccl. 3:1*

WELL-ORDERED DAYS

"It's seemed like Saturday all day to me,"
We say sometimes, half laughing, half annoyed.
Each day is individual, and should be
Itself, in proper order; no employed
And self-respecting Tuesday ought to flaunt
A careless Saturday aspect, to mar
Our most ambitious plans; we never want
To lose our places in the calendar.

Especially there must not be a sign
Of Wednesday bustle or of Friday rush
In spacious, tranquil days when sunbeams shine
With muted gentleness, and breezes hush
Their whisperings, and trees, approving, nod
At Sunday people, taking time for God.

WE THANK THEE, HEAVENLY FATHER, for a day set apart for worship and for rest. We thank thee for release from the tensions of our everyday occupations, for a day when we are free to join in fellowship with thy people to praise thee, to seek thy forgiveness for our failures in love and service, and thy help and guidance through the coming week. May we never forget how much we need thy help; may we never forget that unless we keep one day especially for thee, we soon find that all the days are all awry. Help us come to thee this day, our Father, with open, seeking hearts, that thou mayest go through all the days with us. In our Savior's name. AMEN.

Be doers of the word, and not hearers only, deceiving yourselves.—*Jas.* 1:22

NO HILLS TO CLIMB

Lord, it is easy to desire
That children everywhere
Have hills to climb in summer
And wild rose scented air
To breathe, and fireflies to catch
Gently, and to release,
And always have, upon their brows
Thy radiant peace.

But, Lord, it isn't easy
Sometimes for me to talk
Pleasantly to the sullen boys
Who chase outlaws, and stalk
Indians across my flower beds
Time after thoughtless time.
Lord, keep me patient with each child
Who has no hills to climb.

WE NEED THY HOURLY HELP, O GOD, in the often disconcerting attempt to apply abstract ideals to concrete situations. Thou knowest it is far easier for us to feel a vague benevolence and good will toward people in general than to be truly kind and patient with one irritating person in particular. Help us, Lord, to focus our sympathetic attention on the problems of people near at hand, and if we cannot give them all they need for rewarding living, help us to give at least our personal interest and understanding. In Christ's name. AMEN.

I will lift up mine eyes.—*Ps. 121:1, K.J.V.*
I will arise and go to my father.—*Luke 15:18*
I will hear what God the Lord will speak.—*Ps. 85:8, K.J.V.*

I WILL LIFT UP MINE EYES

Let us be always willing, Lord,
To lift our downcast eyes
Above the baffling mysteries
That always must comprise
Much of our living, day by day,
Above the grievous pain
Of wrongs that men commit, to where
The constant hills remain.

From soaring mountaintops of truth,
From great ideals that tower
In majesty, from human lives
Lived in thy spirit's power—
Forever thou art offering, Lord,
Thy help for every ill;
Yet none can ever receive thy help
Unless he says, "I will."

KEEP US, O GOD, from becoming so dulled in heart by tedious routines, and so despondent in spirit over vexing circumstances, that we lapse into sullen depression, having no strong, determined will to lift our eyes, to hear thy voice, to rise and go to thee, our Father. Keep us aware, Lord, of the danger of being willing to indulge our low moods, lest our will to faithfulness and righteousness become too weak for us to receive thy help in times of urgent need. In Christ's name. AMEN.

MOUNTAIN RAIN

He stood out in the sopping seventh day
Of thick, dull clouds that almost grazed his head.
It seemed to him his mind was getting gray.
"I've got to keep on thinking blue," he said.

He thought of other noons' exultant sweep
Of blue on blue, of other evenings' kind,
Pure, tender blue. These were the thoughts to keep.
He mustn't let the grayness take his mind.

It was an urgent thing he had to do,
A thing he owed his far-off fellow men.
Unless he somehow kept on thinking blue,
The sky might nevermore be blue again.

MAY WE EVER BE AWARE, OUR FATHER, that though we are
not responsible for the color of the sky, we are responsible for
the color of our thoughts and for the effect our expression has
on other people. Thou hast given us brilliant days of vivid sunlight and glorious colors; thou has given us joyous hours of
pleasantness. Help us to think of these with gratitude and with
hope in dismal times of gloom, so that we may be of good
cheer and turn a pleasant and heartening face to those who are
discouraged and repining. In Christ's name. AMEN.

AFTER FAILURE

The careful, unremitting work
I did has not availed.
I gave my best to one large task,
And now I know I failed.

Today I'll do the little things,
The things I can do best.
I'll do the little, easy things
And give my heart a rest.

A dozen little things, well done,
Will lighten failure's sorrow
And give me strength to try, once more,
The larger task, tomorrow.

FATHER IN HEAVEN, help us, when we fail, to fail successfully, without complaints, excuses, or resentments. Teach us that no matter how often we may fail, we are not failures till we cease to try, and that what seems failure in men's eyes may be success in thine. For thou, Lord, knowest all our inward impediments; thou knowest that overcoming these enough to undertake a difficult task may be a form of victory in itself. Grant that each task we try to do may strengthen us and enlarge our capabilities; grant us wisdom to know what work we ought to do, and resolute perseverance in the doing. In Christ's name. AMEN.

With the loyal thou dost show thyself loyal.—*Ps. 18:25*

CONFIDENTIALLY

"Sometimes I think I can't keep on at all.
I can't help wondering what's the use of it,"
Sue said when times were bad. "But I can't say so.
I just can't let Jim down. He'll never quit."

"A dozen times at least," Jim said, "I've thought,
There's no use going on. I'm licked. I'm through.
But Sue—well, she's so spunky all the time.
I just can't say a thing like that to Sue."

That was ten years ago, or maybe nine.
Yes, they came through, of course. They're doing fine.

WE THANK THEE, FATHER, for others' belief in us, for the
trust and loyalty we dare not disappoint. We thank thee for
those whose expectant faith in our good qualities calls forth
more persistent courage than we dreamed that we possessed.
For those who keep us at our best—yet love us at our worst—
we humbly thank thee, Lord. And for all who do not complain,
who bear their burdens quietly, with grace and with good
humor, we ask, O Father, thy victorious aid. In the name of
Christ. AMEN.

What has been is what will be,
and what has been done is what will be done;
and there is nothing new under the sun.

ALL THIS AGAIN

It has all happened before,
The filmy exploring green
That the eye can almost ignore
(But never the heart) on the lean,
Dark rain-glossed branch, and the flourish
Of gold in the old dull grass,
And the robin notes that cherish
All this, this, this.

It has all happened before,
The petal, the leafing bough,
And the airs of the troubadour—
But this is now.

LORD OF THE ORDERLY CHANGES of the seasons, of all the things that have been and will be, we thank thee for loveliness well known yet always new. We thank thee for the sure recurrences of leaves and grass, for the perennial green events on which our hearts rely, yet which amaze us with their freshness when they come. We thank thee that the flowers of every springtime are beautiful as if no flowers had ever bloomed before. We thank thee, Lord, for all life's good, dependable surprises. In Christ's name. AMEN.

Rain in abundance, O God, thou didst shed abroad;
thou didst restore thy heritage as it languished.
—*Ps. 68:9*

ANOTHER SUMMER

Summer was hot and dry, a dragging weight
Of haggard green upon the earth, a tense,
Frustrated expectation that some late
Relenting rain might bring us recompense
For that hard sky that seemed to bruise the eyes
Turned to it wistfully, and for the flowers
Discouraged in each petaled enterprise,
Like all our hopes, by heavy, dust-thick hours.

But autumn brought the rain—oh, autumn brought
Such innocent translucencies of blue,
Such gentle atmospheres as we had thought
The summer would. In autumn days we knew
An interval of grace beyond belief,
Another summer, beautiful and brief.

LORD, GIVE US GRACE to trust thee in the arid fruitless seasons.
Strengthen our hearts, O Father, in the times of dusty discouragement, when our hopes wither and our best aspirations and efforts come to nothing. Keep us in uncomplaining obedience to thy will, and after the time of testing, grant us to rejoice again in the fullness of thy blessing. In Christ's name.
AMEN.

Who are these that fly like a cloud,
and like doves to their windows?

—Isa. 60:8

EIGHT PIGEONS

I do not know why pigeons flew
About a sky of listless gray
As if it were exultant blue,
As if this were a golden day.

I know they swept around, around,
With swift co-ordinated ease.
I do not know what joy they found
Above the tops of barren trees.

I know that I shall never know
What lilting impulse made them fly,
But having seen them doing so
I have no need of knowing why.

WE ARE THANKFUL, LORD, for every unexpected glimpse of gladness. We are thankful for the grace of small surprises, which restore a sense of pleasant wonder to our hearts in dismal weather. We are grateful for all that lifts our eyes and our spirits from dullness, for all that quickens us and brings us new awareness and delight. AMEN.

These all look to thee,
to give them their food in due season.
When thou givest to them, they gather it up;
when thou openest thy hand, they are filled with
good things.

—*Ps. 104:27-28*

RESOURCES

Across brown fields
The sparrows go
Flying quickly,
Flying low.

Within brown fields
The sparrows find
Refreshment suited
To each mind.

They cluster happily
On thistles
And offer thanks
With chirps and whistles.

How fortunate
For their own needs
That sparrows feel
No scorn for weeds.

FATHER IN HEAVEN, grant that in our times of need we may
not overlook or fail to use the resources available to us. Grant
us to trust faithfully that help will come from thee, who knowest all our needs before we ask; and make us willing to receive
it, though it comes in unexpected ways, by humble means.
Keep our hearts and minds flexible and resilient, willing to
adjust cheerfully to changing circumstances, and grateful for
all the help that we receive. AMEN.

There be many that say, Who will shew us any good? Lord, lift thou up the light of thy countenance upon us. Thou hast put gladness in my heart, more than in the time that their corn and their wine increased.—*Ps. 4:6-7, K.J.V.*

DECEMBER SONG

Outside the world is dreary,
Outside the world is bare,
But in my heart is gladness;
God has put gladness there.

I think of shepherds watching
Upon a starlit hill.
I think of songs proclaiming
God's glory and good will.

Oh, sing the joyful tidings
Till all have understood
God's will for men is gladness,
God's will for men is good.

We thank thee, heavenly father, for gladness that does not depend on outward things, for gladness welling up within our hearts because of what thou art and what thou wouldest have us be. We pray for all who have not known this saving gladness, and for all who in bleak skepticism or careless frivolity or wrong pursuits have lost the inward music of thy grace. Grant to them all, O God, belief in thy eternal mercy, and joyous obedience to thy holy will. Through Christ our Lord. amen.

For God alone my soul waits in silence.—*Ps. 62:1*

PRAYER IN QUIETNESS

Lord of deep quietness,
Now, with none near,
I bring to thy silence
All whom I hold dear;

All those who are jostled
And deafened by din,
Losing in loudness
Thy presence within;

Lord, touch with thy calmness
Each clamorous heart,
Receiving them into
This peace where thou art.

O let this joyous
Deep silence of prayer
Hush now with its wonder
All hearts everywhere.

DEAR HEAVENLY FATHER, in reverent awe we praise thee for the enriching fellowship of prayer. We thank thee for the privilege of praying for those who are especially dear to us, and for those who are especially in need of thy healing presence and restoring power. Help us always, Lord, to pray with purity of purpose, with fervent spirits and responsible hearts for our friends, our enemies, and for all people. In Christ's name. AMEN.

Thus says the Lord:
>Stand by the roads, and look,
>>and ask for the ancient paths,
>where the good way is; and walk in it,
>>and find rest for your souls.

—Jer. 6:16

PEDESTRIAN

To be pedestrian is to be
Profoundly intimate
With earth scent and grass sheen
And the sun's light and weight.

It's scorched dust and brambles
And pebbles in the shoe,
And violets surprising
The near, perceptive view.

Oh, wings are wildly lovely
In blue, alluring sky,
But who would live at standstill
Because he cannot fly?

WE THANK THEE, HEAVENLY FATHER, that thou hast shown us the ancient paths of righteousness, and that thou leadest us continually in the way. We thank thee for all thy encouragement when we have stumbled, for all thy patience when we have been laggard and have grumbled at the roughness of the way. We thank thee, Lord, for teaching us that only as we walk with thee do we advance at all; that the smoothest way without thee is a way of nothingness, and the rockiest way with thee is a way of peace and rest. We thank thee in Christ's name. AMEN.

IV

THROUGH THE VALLEY

VI

THROUGH THE VALLEY

Yea, though I walk through the valley of the shadow of death, I will fear no evil: for thou art with me; thy rod and thy staff they comfort me.—*Ps. 23:4, K.J.V.*

THROUGH THE VALLEY

I love the brown December earth,
I love the gray December sky,
The calm acceptances of dearth
Without complaint or question why
The bird has left the barren bough,
Or why the bough should be left bare,
Or why the field is empty now
And open to the piercing air.

I love the grave simplicity
Of faith that, acquiescent, still,
Abides the tempest, tranquilly
Obedient to the Father's will.
I love to know that, yielded thus,
The saving Christ may come to us.

STRENGTHEN OUR FAITH, LORD, that however heavily the shadows darken about us in the valleys of bereavement and trouble, we need not travel the lonely way alone. Help us trust that though many evils thicken across our way, we need not fear whatever comes to us. For thou art with us, Lord; thou art ever with us: though in the numbness of our misery we may be unable to feel thy presence, thou art with us nevertheless. We thank thee, Lord, that when we yield our suffering hearts to thee in humble trust, the deep assurance of thy presence, and the healing of thy comfort, comes to us. In Christ's name. AMEN.

For God hath not given us the spirit of fear; but of power, and of love, and of a sound mind.—*Tim. 1:7, K.J.V.*

THE HEALING MESSAGE

Our God is very patient with our fears.
He understands our dread of loss and change,
And ever to his people, through the years,
Whenever anything is new and strange,
"Fear not," the healing message comes again
That came to Abraham in the oak tree's shade,
To prophets, kings, and ordinary men,
"Fear not, I am thy God; be not dismayed."

"Why are you fearful?" Jesus asked his friends.
However great our task or hard our lot,
Beset with questions no one comprehends,
Our hearts may hear him saying still, "Fear not,
O little flock"; and, trusting him, may find
The spirit of power and love and a sound mind.

FOR ALL THY PATIENCE with our weaknesses, we thank thee, heavenly Father, and for thy continuous reassurances to all who are of a fearful heart. We thank thee that thou ever bidest us be of good courage and of good cheer. We thank thee for making available to us the spirit of power: power to do and to endure, power to love thee and others in all circumstances, power to think reasonably and constructively about our problems as they arise. May we constantly appropriate and use this power, that it may increase more and more. In Christ's name. AMEN.

When Jesus saw her weeping, and the Jews who came with her also weeping, he was deeply moved in spirit and troubled . . . . Jesus wept.—*John 11:33, 35*

IN SYMPATHY

I know that all is different for you now.
There is a strangeness in the earth and sky
And all familiar things when one we love
Is dead. We look at those who did not die
With wonder, and at those who are not sad
Uncomprehendingly. I know, I know,
When hearts have followed loved ones to the grave
Return to life is difficult and slow.

Oh, in the lonely strangeness, feel it true
There is no difference in my love for you.

O GOD, FATHER MOST MERCIFUL, who knowest all our sorrows, who art touched by all our distresses, we pray with aching hearts for those who are separated from the familiar goodness of life by the unbelievable strangeness of new grief. We have known the sad bewilderment and the lonely alienation from living, Lord, and we know that there is little we can do to help the grieving heart resume its wonted ways, except to make our love a constant prayer. We claim for them thy promise, Lord, that thou wilt never leave us or forsake us; we pray that they may be aware of thy presence sustaining and guiding them through the hard days of learning how to live with loss. Help them, O God, trustfully to relinquish their loved one to thy keeping and their sorrow to thy comfort. In the name of Christ, who wept for the sorrows of his friends. AMEN.

Unto them that mourn in Zion, to give unto them beauty for ashes.—*Isa. 61:3, K.J.V.*

GLIMPSED

I had not thought of being glad again.
I can endure the opening of each day,
Do small tasks in an ordinary way,
And bear the nights, each night as long as ten.
And I can read the words that people pen
In sympathy, see visitors, and say
The right words, even asking them to stay,
And smile a little, every now and then.

This seemed as much as I could ever do.
To see beyond the doing of these things
Required a vision that I never had.
But when I glimpsed a bird just now, there flew
Across my heart, like fugitive wild wings,
The possibility of being glad.

THOU KNOWEST, LORD, that when grief is raw and new, we feel that grief is all we can ever feel again. We thank thee for whatever stirs our hearts from mere endurance, for little customary things that make us feel at home with life once more. When there is no return to us of one we love, help us, O God, to make the most of what remains. Grant that we may not shrink from entering into new relationships lest we be hurt again; help us to keep our hearts open to give and to receive affection with greater sympathy and gentleness than we had known before. In Christ's name. AMEN.

Now the boy . . . continued to grow both in stature and in favor with the Lord and with men—*I Sam.* 2:26

A BOY GROWN TALL

He climbed the steepest hilltops
That thrust into the skies,
A boy grown tall with laughter,
With summer in his eyes.

Too speedily, too swiftly,
His earthly summit won,
He climbed the final mountain
That leans into the sun.

But oh, when skies are laughing,
I think I see him still
Standing, tall as summer,
On this steep hill.

WE THANK THEE, HEAVENLY FATHER, for all who were lovely and pleasant in their lives. We thank thee for those who made earth and sky and all of life more meaningful to us by their glad zest for living and achieving. We thank thee for the continuing inspiration of their lives. Through our poignant missing of their presence here with us we thank thee for faith that they are growing still, our Father, in thy favor, with all joy. In Christ's name. AMEN.

As for man, his days are like grass;
    he flourishes like a flower of the field;
for the wind passes over it, and it is gone,
    and its place knows it no more.
But the steadfast love of the Lord is from ever-
    lasting to everlasting
upon those who fear him.

—*Ps. 103:15-17*

EACH WINTER

Even while the bright leaves darken on the ground
And skies grow heavy and the cold wind shrills
Across the earth, and sullen raindrops pound,
Our hearts are sure of spring and daffodils.

And yet, our hearts are wistful, now and then.
Each winter some plants freeze, some great trees fall.
We know that April always comes again;
We know that April never comes to all.

So TEACH US TO NUMBER OUR DAYS, O FATHER, that we may apply our hearts unto wisdom. Teach us especially the gentle wisdom of treasuring well those whom we love, and all those with whom we have to do, while there is time and opportunity. Help us, in spite of reticence and shyness, to express our feeling for them spontaneously and naturally, to make them sure of our affection while we may. Soften to us the lonely Aprils, Lord, when we can no longer share with our dearest ones the glowing loveliness of earth and sky. May gratitude for Aprils we have shared sustain us till they share with us a lovelier land than April's. In Christ's name. AMEN.

A gentle tongue is a tree of life,
   but perverseness in it breaks the spirit.

—*Prov. 15:4*

OF CERTAIN WORDS

Water must ripple
When stones are cast
Into its depths.
Calm comes, at last
When the last circumference
Of dismay
Is spent. Calm comes;
But the stones stay.

THOU KNOWEST, LORD, the turmoil words can cause, and the unceasing burden they can be. Grant, of thy mercy, that when others speak hurting words of us, we may not be tempted to retaliate. Help us to wait in silence till we can decide calmly whether their criticisms are justified; help us to profit from whatever truth we hear, however hard it may be to accept. And help us to be careful and gentle, Lord, in all the words we say, remembering how easily words can be misunderstood, and how irreparable may be the hurt that even well-intended words can cause. In Christ's name. AMEN.

I had fainted, unless I had believed to see the goodness of the Lord in the land of the living.—*Ps. 27:13, K.J.V.*

KNOWN ROOM

A known room is the place for being ill.
Worn books upon a wide familiar shelf
And tended plants upon a window sill
Remind one of a vigorous healthy self
Who took delight in thoughts and things that grow,
Who had decisions of one's own to make,
Had much to learn and something to bestow
And was not merely one anonymous ache.

Always the wandering, fever-puzzled mind,
The pain-bewildered, dazed identity,
Needs these reminders if one is to find
The way to what one was, and meant to be,
From alien depths where only strangers dwell.
A known room is the place for getting well.

HEAVENLY FATHER, may steadfast faith in thee and in thy present help be so deep a part of us that it will sustain us even in hours of weakness and unconsciousness. Grant that our occupations and interests in days of health may be such as offer incentive to recovery in days of illness. And grant that we may use the days of recovery from illness, whether they be long or short, for rediscovering the values that hold real meaning for our lives, and for rededicating our strength to thee and to the fulfilling of thy purposes for us. In Christ's name. AMEN.

Thou hast given me room when I was in distress.—Ps. 4:1

RECOVERY

It wasn't that I hadn't seen the sky
And earth for months. I saw it all through glass,
But hard transparencies can foil the eye
With sparkle, and when brilliant sunbeams pass
And dark looks in where sunbeams
   danced and whirled,
Then glass shows one himself and not the world.

The hour they wheeled me out beneath the bare
Astounding distances of blue, I saw
Colors of things untouched by glassy glare,
And used light words to them against my awe—
Against my heart's embarrassing demand
To tell them things they couldn't understand.

WE THANK THEE, HEAVENLY FATHER, for the inexpressible joy of rediscovering the beauty of thy world when we have been long shut away from it. We thank thee for the poignant privilege of seeing with new eyes the ordinary miracles of earth and sky, and of rejoicing in the simple verity of things. We pray, O God, that thou wilt hasten the recovery of those who are shut in by cramping walls from the enlarging, spacious glory of the sky; we pray thy richest blessings on the people who work with thee to set them free. In Christ's name. AMEN.

And the glorious beauty, which is on the head of the fat valley, shall be a fading flower.—*Isa. 28:4, K.J.V.*

SPRING FREEZE

Through the clear, balmy, blossom-scented air
The broadcast warning comes to us: "Hard cold
Is on the way. Go gather in, with care,
Whatever you would keep of pink and gold.
All that is blooming now will die tonight.
Nothing can stop this onward-coming freeze
From killing with its swift, invisible blight
All hope of fruit on all the flowering trees."

Mutely we gather jonquils, violets,
Japonica, forsythia, one spray
Of apple blossoms, thinking of the debts
We counted on the apple crop to pay.
We gather what we can of spring to keep,
And, being farmer folk, we do not weep.

WE KNOW, O GOD, that none of us can be immune to unexpected loss and swift disaster. We know that our most provident, far-seeing plans for our future may fail, through no fault of our own, and that the fruit of years of careful, conscientious work may be swept away in an instant. But grant that we may not live in fear of such events; grant that we may not set our hearts upon material blessings nor base our security on outward things. Help us rather to choose the good part that cannot be taken from us, the habits of abiding faith in thee, of undeviating integrity, of cheerfulness and friendliness and love. AMEN.

Thou waterest its furrows abundantly,
   settling its ridges,
softening it with showers,
   and blessing its growth.

—*Ps. 65:10*

RENEWAL

This summer, flowers are very few
Because of sudden cold in spring,
But frequent, gentle rains renew
Earth after three dry years, and bring
So deep a pleasure in the scent
And radiance of little showers
That few remember to lament
The many-colored hosts of flowers,
As with contented eyes we see
What hearts forget as dry years pass:
How gently blue the sky can be,
How freshly green the leaves and grass.

WE THANK THEE, HEAVENLY FATHER, that though the blossoms die, the trees remain. We thank thee that in spite of frost and drought and flood the earth abides, and that crops can be replanted and cities can be rebuilt. We thank thee for the constant hope within the hearts of men, rising triumphant over their disasters. And we thank thee for the power, O God, by which lives that seem irreparably blighted are enabled to bring forth the fruits of thy spirit—love, joy, and peace. AMEN.

BARREN HILL

Once there was beauty on this barren hill;
A tree stood here and wrestled with the sky.
Angry and stubborn, challenging the weather,
It battled for its being with a wry
Tenacious wrath against all easy growing,
Against all pliant, yielding ways of life.
It fought the rain. It grappled with the storm.
It beat against the wind in swirling strife.
Almost it made its native earth a foe,
Scorning the scanty sustenance it drew
From rocky contradiction. Friendless, free,
Fed by its own integrity it grew.

A lightning blast defeated it. The blaze
Shriveled the sky as the fierce stroke descended.
Now bland suns beam upon the barren hill,
On vacant emptiness, all beauty ended.

HEAVENLY FATHER, keep us from easy yieldings to the winds of circumstance. Keep us from timid conformity to prevailing opinions, when to conform involves any sacrifice of principle. Keep us from compromising our convictions; keep us from doing what we believe is wrong even though it may be the accepted, popular thing to do. Keep us from assenting by silence to slanderous prejudice and bigotry lest we be thought peculiar if we speak. Help us at any cost, at any risk, to champion the things that we believe are right. Help us to withstand in the evil day, and having done all, to stand—or to go down in triumph to defeat. AMEN.

Thou dost keep him in perfect peace,
  whose mind is stayed on thee,
  because he trusts in thee.

—Isa. 26:3

ALL THIS DAY

God of eternal glory, keep my heart.
O keep my heart stayed on thee all this day,
And if my old hurts ache and new tears start,
Let me remember these will pass away.
Let me remember pain is not forever
And grief and loneliness will finally cease,
But thou abidest, and no power can sever
Thy people from thy love and joy and peace.

Thy love, O Father, reaching out to all
Earth's wearily bewildered ones; thy joy
In costly loving that seeks to recall
Storm-shattered lives to peace without alloy—
Let everyone I meet find these in me
This day; O keep my heart stayed, Lord, on thee.

WE THANK THEE, LORD, for thy great promises. We ask thy necessary help to make thy promises effective in our lives. Forgive us for the faithless hours when our minds focus dismally on worries, griefs, and fears instead of being stayed on thee in peace. Help us to practice faithfully day by day, and hour by hour, the quiet staying of our hearts on thee, who art eternally greater than our hearts or any sorrows of our passing days. In Christ's name. AMEN.

The Lord will give grace and glory.—*Ps. 84:11, K.J.V.*

FOR ALL THE GLORY

For every April day of gloom and glory
I thank thee, Lord; for every April day
When storm clouds swathe the world in transitory,
Swift, violent darkness, till a sudden ray
Of dazzling light illuminates the fresh
New buds and leaves adrift in silvery air,
And rainbows, slowly shining forth, enmesh
Our hearts in all the beauty they can bear.

Dear Lord, I thank thee for such days as this
More than for any others I have known,
Days of all earthly days I would not miss.
I thank thee for the sullen storm clouds blown
Across the sky, for silver-misted bloom—
For all the glory, and for all the gloom.

WE THANK THEE, HEAVENLY FATHER, for light that rises in
the darkness, and for the darkness that makes us realize how
lovely is the light. Thou knowest our hearts, O God: thou
knowest we would not choose the darkness or the storm; we
would not choose the valley of the shadow; we would avoid
all sorrow if we could. We thank thee, Lord, that out of the
experiences from which we shrink, we learn the glory of light,
the comfort of thy presence, and the sufficiency of thy consola-
tions. We thank thee in Christ's name. AMEN.

V

THOU PREPAREST A TABLE

Thou preparest a table before me in the presence of mine enemies: thou anointest my head with oil; my cup runneth over—*Ps. 23:5, K.J.V.*

THOU PREPAREST A TABLE

We thank thee for all tables well prepared
With every necessary sustenance;
Each table where our daily bread is shared
With our sustaining friends; for each expanse
Of provident wide fields and ample sky
Spread out before us with a good array
Of varied shapes and hues that satisfy
Our needs for food and beauty, day by day.

Remember tables, Lord, where there is want
Of these essential blessings, where dark fears
Of bitter enemies harass and daunt
The hearts that eat their bitter bread with tears.
Grant freedom to all people, that the whole
Rich joy of life be theirs, when none offends
And thou preparest for each human soul
A table in the presence of his friends.

FATHER IN HEAVEN, we know that not only in other lands but in our own land there are many who, because of the enmity of their neighbors, cannot peacefully enjoy the sustaining blessings of life. Grant, Lord, that we may never be reconciled to this knowledge. Grant that we may never complacently accept as our due the blessings given us, so long as prejudice denies these blessings to others. May we ever pray fervently and work faithfully for the freeing of human beings from human oppression. In Christ's name. AMEN.

I spread out my hands all the day
    to ·a rebellious people, . . .
who say, "Keep to yourself,
    do not come near me, for I am set apart from you."
                              —*Isa.* 65:2, 5

THE CAPTIVE CHILDREN

There are pink and white children,
Peach petal children,
With hair like waves of light from the morning sun
And eyes the young blue of the dawn sky.

And there are brown and golden children,
Autumn oak leaf children,
With hair and eyes
Bright-dark as midnight heavens.

There are those who say to the peach petal children,
"We will keep you safe.
We will dull the eager luster of dark eyes;
We will see that the sky-dark eyes turn
   always earthward,
Respectfully, submissively, gratefully.
We will teach them that the open sky,
The upward look, the dawn,
Are only for you."

Perhaps these do not know that they are saying
To the children with morning eyes,
"We will keep you safe
In dungeons of hate and fear."

HAVE PITY, LORD, on those who teach children to despise one
another, and grant that children of all races may learn good
ways of life together. AMEN.

82

BEFORE DEPARTURE

Let us who pioneer
On any neighboring star
Ponder with seemly fear
Things that are not, and are.

The Indians, harried, cheated,
The passenger pigeons, slain,
Are not. The raw, depleted
Eroded lands remain.

Lest birds of Pollux perish
Upon our swift advent,
Let us resolve to cherish
The strange, the different—

Resolve the worlds that lure us
Shall not, for luring, lose
The blossoms of Arcturus,
The trees of Betelgeuse.

We have not been empowered,
We have not dreamed and toiled
For Sirius deflowered,
Aldebaran despoiled.

LORD, WE REJOICE in the adventurous courage of men's minds, for we believe that the urge to dare, explore, and know is of thy giving. But we remember with deep penitence the havoc men have wrought on earth, and the evils they visit on their fellow men. And we beseech thee, O God, that whether or not it is given men to reach the distant stars, they may be enabled of thy grace to behave with courtesy and reverence, as people who themselves are native to a star. AMEN.

Thou dost cause the grass to grow for the cattle,
　　and plants for man to cultivate,
that he may bring forth food from the earth,

．　　．　　．　　．　　．　　．　　．　　．

　　and bread to strengthen man's heart.

—*Ps. 104:14, 15*

UNHUNGERING

Again the land lies dreaming under haze,
Idle a little while, its ancient task
Of nurture done once more, with the wide gaze
Of sky approving all. The orchards bask
In warm contentment, and the garnered fields
Rest tranquilly. And casual on a low
Fence post, a child surveys the land that shields
Him from a lack whose name he does not know,
Enjoying tangy apple butter spread
Lavishly on an ample slice of bread.

WE THANK THEE, LORD, for the richness of our land, and for the faithful work of those who sow and cultivate and reap, making our lives secure from the threat of hunger. And we pray for all the people of earth whose lives are not secure, whose days are passed in the hard struggle for mere subsistence, with little of human dignity and joy. We are grateful for all that is being done to help the people of the hungry nations help themselves to richer lives; but we are shamed, Lord, by the knowledge that it is not enough. Forgive us for our negligence and selfishness, for our preoccupation with acquiring luxuries for ourselves while other people lack life's bare essentials. Stir up our hearts, O God, to genuine concern and sacrificial giving. In Christ's name. AMEN.

> She rises while it is yet night
> and provides food for her household.
>
> —*Prov. 31:15*

A WOMAN'S WAY

When her teen-age daughter
Has a broken heart,
A woman sets to baking
A luscious cherry tart.

When her son's team loses,
When his dog is dead,
A woman bakes a chocolate cake
Or spicy gingerbread.

When the crops are scanty,
When the bills are high,
A woman smiles her brightest
And bakes an apple pie.

Sympathy for sorrow,
Solace for mistakes,
Go into the mixing
When a woman bakes.

FATHER IN HEAVEN, we thank thee for all the warmhearted, sympathetic people who sustain the hearts of their families and friends with their affectionate understanding. We thank thee for all who give comfort and cheer in daily, taken-for-granted ways. Uphold them, Lord, in the unending small demands of living, and grant them the fruit of their hands, the blessing, praise, and honor of those they love and serve. In Christ's name. AMEN.

At evening time there shall be light.—*Zech. 14:7*

FAMILY VIEW

Three of us view this land we know,
Severely contoured, winter bare,
In atmosphere of afterglow
Without a shadow anywhere.

Three of us pleasuring our eyes
In clarity, our glances meet
And almost shyly recognize
A moment perfect and complete.

Not something that we need discuss,
Joy is, without a why or how,
If not for others, yet for us,
If not for always, yet for now.

FOR GENTLE TIMES of unspoken communion with one another, we thank thee, our Father. We cherish gratefully all unmarred moments of loveliness and peace that we have shared with people dear to us. May there be many moments of quiet grace for all families, Lord, after the rush and hurry of the day. And may the gracious memory of beauty shared with loved ones give each of us more understanding to share with everyone whom we may meet. In Christ's name. AMEN.

Bless the Lord, O my soul;
    and all that is within me, bless his holy name!
Bless the Lord, O my soul,
    and forget not all his benefits.

—Ps. 103:1-2

SO MANY BENEFITS

"Forget not all his benefits." There is
No memory so exact it can retain,
Unceasingly, the constant thought of his
Perpetual mercies: earth and sun and rain,
Small unexpected blossoms, endless sky,
Good friends to share our laughter and our tears,
Forgiveness when our lives are all awry,
And healing for our illnesses and fears.

So many benefits of grace to each,
Not all can be remembered. Oh, but let
Us not forget them all, while we beseech
Some special gift, complaining with regret.
Bless him for every blessing we recall;
Forget not all his benefits—not all.

FORGIVE US, OUR FATHER, for often forgetting all the multi-
tude of thy blessings to us. Our memories are faulty and our
hearts more faulty still. Lord, we would change our minds and
change our hearts. We would remember faithfully what thou
hast done, and offer thanks; we would remember reverently
what thou art, and offer praise; we would worship thee and
bless thee in sincerity and truth. In Christ's name. AMEN.

BETWEEN THE LINES

I smile at finding leaves or flowers pressed
Between the pages of a well-worn book
Loaned by a friend, for always they suggest
Good outdoor hours when friendly breezes shook
Bright leaves across an open page, bestowing
The kindly confirmation of a tree
Upon the thoughts expressed there, with
   whose growing
Within the mind, the elements agree.

And even if the leaf or flower were placed
There merely for safekeeping, being brought
To the book from out of doors, it still is graced
With meaning, since it proves my friend well taught
In the fine art of keeping lovely hours
Preserved in fragile forms of leaves and flowers.

GOD OF ALL TRUTH, we thank thee for the good treasures of knowledge and wisdom that are available in books, and for the friends who share these treasures with us. We thank thee for all the pleasant learning hours we have spent with books that filled some special need. We thank thee for books that help our minds encompass some truth before unrealized, that help our hearts to sympathize with the problems of people whose lands and situations are different from ours, and that deepen our sense of fellowship with all humanity. For all the good, enriching books and for those who write them, we thank thee, Father, in Christ's name. AMEN.

GOOD RETURN

When books come home from visiting a friend,
The welcome they receive is even more
Cordial than any greeting I extend
To books come fresh with newness from a store.
For now there is the certainty of pleasure,
Not promise merely; eagerly I find
The pages rich with known, familiar treasure,
The special sentences I underlined.

And there is deeper meaning in each thought
That I have pondered well, since it has found
Response within a wise friend's mind, and brought
Him understanding. Any book is bound
To be a better friend for being part
Of people who are native to my heart.

WE ARE GRATEFUL, LORD, for the rewarding interchange of
thoughts and experiences that keeps our minds alert to many
of the various aspects of truth. May our choice of books ever
be such that we can confidently share them with the people
whose opinion we value. May our reading be not only for
pleasure and relaxation, but in the spirit of the one who said,
"You will know the truth, and the truth will make you free."
In his name. AMEN.

I thank my God in all my remembrance of you.—Phil. 1:3

NOTE TO A FRIEND

There is not time, now, in the crowded years,
For the immediate acknowledgment
Of friendship's thoughtfulness; a letter sent
In understanding of an hour when tears
Oppressed the heart, or any letter sharing
A good experience fully, or a small
Gift sent "because it looks like you," and all
The little acts that testify of caring.

But though we have not leisure now to pen
Our heart's response as quickly as we could
In earlier days, and that response was good
To have, we are as fortunate now as then;
For now we have this satisfying glow
Because, without the need of words, we know.

FATHER IN HEAVEN, we thank thee for the trusted friends on whom our hearts rely. We thank thee for the steadfast warmth of their affection through the years. We thank thee for the constant hearts that do not criticize or blame our inadequacies but, fully understanding, love us still. We remember with deep gratitude our happy hours of good companionship with them, the delight of meeting after absence, and the comfort of knowing that in the longest absence we are faithfully remembered. We thank thee, Father, for the gift, beyond our meriting, of loyal friends. In Christ's name. AMEN.

Very pleasant have you been to me;
your love to me was wonderful.

—*II Sam.* 1:26

NOT LESS THAN STARS

I'm glad that in this friendship there can be
A quiet sense of continuity,
A sureness that if we forget, today,
Some tidings, some good word we meant to say,
There will be many other times for sharing
Our thoughts, and for a deep untroubled caring.

This friendship has a constancy that stills
Our hearts with peace, like forests and old hills,
A sense of something that goes on and on;
Nor do we prize it less than stars, than dawn.

WE PRAY FOR THY CONTINUING BLESSINGS, LORD, upon each friend who is a blessing to our lives. We ask for them abundant health of soul and body, joyous tranquillity in all relationships, prosperity and good success in worthy undertakings. We pray that thou wilt guard them from all evil, and that thou wilt guard us from hurting them in any way. Help us to be responsive to their needs, sensitive to their moods, and deeply loyal to the best in them. Most of all, may we never cease to pray for them that they may increase and abound in the knowledge and love of Christ. In his name. AMEN.

Do not withhold good from those to whom it is due,
when it is in your power to do it.

—*Prov.* 3:27

ON EXPRESSING THANKS

God, being always near, receives
Immediate thanks for many a thing
That lights my heart: rainshine on leaves,
And the way chickadees expertly swing
On sunflower heads, and the certain way
Help comes, and light, when all is dim.
I need not cross the town to say
My thanks, nor write a note to him.

But the new friend whom I seldom meet,
The stranger who has made earth better,
Unless I travel down his street
Or write my praises in a letter,
May halt, discouraged, unrenewed,
And never guess my gratitude.

GIVE US, HEAVENLY FATHER, hearts quick to respond to the good that people do, whether to us or to others. Help us to make the extra effort needed to express tactfully and sincerely our appreciation of an unselfish act, a courageous stand against popular evils, a lonely struggle against adversity. Help us to seek for the disregarded excellences in the hearts and lives of others, and to encourage them by words of genuine praise. Give us, Lord, the tongue of those who are taught, that we may know how to sustain with a word those who are weary. In Christ's name. AMEN.

Who can utter the mighty doings of the Lord,
or show forth all his praise?
Blessed are they who observe justice,
who do righteousness at all times!

—*Ps. 106:2-3*

IN HIS PRAISE

I need to offer thanks with every hour,
Lest I be overwhelmed at daylight's end
Not having time to mention some bright flower
That pleased my sight, or some good word a friend
Sent for my help, or some quite unexpected
Chuckle of pure delight a small girl brought.
Lest some beloved blessing seem neglected,
I need to offer thanks with every thought.

But if I would more perfectly express
My thanks for all God is, beyond, above,
His daily gifts; for mercy, righteousness,
And patient, seeking, undefeated love,
I need to make each act of all my days
An act of loving service, in his praise.

ETERNAL GOD of righteousness and glory, lift thou our hearts to awe and adoration. Teach us to reverence thee, O God, so deeply that if all the little blessings of our days should be withdrawn, we still would praise thee with devoted hearts for thy own being. Grant us in all circumstances entirely to trust in thy perfect goodness, thy infinite wisdom, and thy steadfast love, and to praise thee with all we are and with all we do. In Christ's name. AMEN.

> Open to me the gates of righteousness,
>   that I may enter through them
>   and give thanks to the Lord.

—Ps. 118:19

THESE ARE MY THANKS

These are my thanks, Lord: not my words alone
Or the quick lifting of my heart to thee
In silence when a sudden wind has blown
A gust of gold from some October tree,
Or when I've seen a customary view
Transfigured by a whirling mist of stars,
Or watched with grateful eyes the earth made new
By spring's perennial mercies on its scars.

But more than these, the little gentle things
I try to do to ease an aching heart,
Or give some trembling, wounded spirit wings—
Lord, they are very small, but they are part
Of the deep gratitude of all my days.
They are my fervent thanks, my ardent praise.

ACCEPT, O GOD, our small imperfect service, and use it for thy glory and the fulfillment of thy purposes in human lives. Help us, our Father, to abide in thee, to grow daily more responsive to thy guidance, more quick to know what thou wouldest have us do, more able to do it in the way we should. Thou who hast given us abundantly of thyself and of thy blessings, give us the grace of sharing with others, gently and lovingly, the joy and gladness thou hast given us. In the name of Christ. AMEN.

VI

GOODNESS AND MERCY

Surely goodness and mercy shall follow me all the days of my life; and I will dwell in the house of the Lord for ever.
—*Ps. 23:6, K.J.V.*

GOODNESS AND MERCY SHALL FOLLOW ME

Let me remember, as the old year ends,
That there has been no year without some new
And unexpected goodness that transcends
The years; let me recall how friendships grew
In days that then appeared so desolate
That nothing beautiful could ever grow
In them; and let me not forget how great,
Good mercies came when hope had seemed to go.

Oh, let me not forget, beginning now
A year that holds few promises of good,
That even the darkest years contained, somehow,
More joyous days than I dared hope they could;
For so I am assured that there will be
Goodness and mercy ever following me.

WE THANK THEE, HEAVENLY FATHER, for blessings of the past and of the future. We trust in thy proven goodness and thy tested mercy, Lord, to bring good out of whatever exacting circumstances we must face. As the bleak days of the past yet held, unknown to us, the beginnings of better things, so will the hard days of the future do. And so we thank thee, Lord of all our days, for all the good that is and is to be. In Christ's name. AMEN.

> I am thy passing guest,
>   a sojourner, like all my fathers.

—*Ps. 39:12*

GUEST

I would live politely
On this pleasant sphere,
Giving due thanks nightly
For my dwelling here;

Admiring every treasure,
Enjoying all that's done
Kindly, for my pleasure,
Underneath the sun;

Courteous to all others
Who are guests with me,
Heedful that another's
Heart be glad and free;

Responsive to each small request
And faithful to each post,
Like the well-conducted guest
Of a gracious host.

O GOD, FORGIVE US, thy passing guests, our often graceless manners. Forgive us for forgetting thee, our host, and behaving as if this wide and various place of our sojourning were ours to devastate and plunder as we will. Forgive us for our frequent callous rudeness to those who, like ourselves, are thy guests upon this earth. Make us aware, Lord, of our many sins against thy hospitality, and enable us to mend our ways. In Christ's name. AMEN.

Count it all joy, my brethren, when you meet various trials, for you know that the testing of your faith produces steadfastness. And let steadfastness have its full effect, that you may be perfect and complete, lacking in nothing.—*Jas. 1:2-4*

WISH

All earth and sky to rest you
And give you peace within—
And challenges to test you,
And struggles you must win.

Someone who shares your singing,
Someone who understands
Your silences—and clinging
To you, pale asking hands,

Till you are patient longer;
For so your heart shall stir
With joy that you are stronger
Than you could dream you were.

MAY WE BE WILLING, LORD, to become strong. We know that strength of body and of soul is gained through exercise and discipline, and not through ease and idleness. We know that faculties which are not used grow useless very soon. And yet we shrink from testing and exertion, from any unusual hard demand upon our strength and faith and patience. God of all goodness, who knowest our natures, grant us to be victorious in all the trials we meet. In Christ's name. AMEN.

Thou makest the outgoings of the morning and the evening
to shout for joy.

—Ps. 65:8

CHANTICLEER

With morning in his burnished throat
He mounts the gatepost to proclaim
The tidings of returning light,
The news of sun in notes of flame.

Against the dark distrusting silence
He shrills that splendor has begun.
Listen! You hear daylight resounding
Across the sky! You hear the sun!

Unfortunate all the folk who slumber
In houses shuttered and withdrawn,
And never hear the cock of morning,
The clarion cock who utters dawn!

WE THANK THEE, HEAVENLY FATHER, for the exultant joy
with which thy creatures greet the coming of each day. We
thank thee for the morning songs of birds rejoicing in the soft,
clear light of dawn. Grant us to greet each day alertly, Lord,
with glad expectancy, never with boredom and an unawakened
mind. At every day's beginning may we praise thee for the
shining gift of light, for the priceless gift of sight, for all the
good endowments of our days. And in the radiance of the
morning may we fix our hearts on thee and on the steadfast
doing of thy will for us, that the gladness of thy presence may
go with us all the day. In Christ's name. AMEN.

Who hath despised the day of small things?—*Zech.* 4:10, K.J.V.

ESSENCE

I shall not remember,
Exactly, the way
The small events happened
That made a good day.

A letter, a visit,
An excellent book,
A rose-silver evening,
A child's special look.

Precise circumstances
Thoughts seldom retain;
But the memory of gladness—
This will remain.

WE THANK THEE, HEAVENLY FATHER, for the little satisfactions of the days that give us memories of pleasantness and goodness. Help us to live each day in gentleness and thoughtfulness of others, so that our deeds may contribute to giving them memories of gladness. May we act promptly on each impulse to friendliness and helpfulness we feel, lest a happy memory be lost because of our delay or diffidence. In Christ's name. AMEN.

Look at the heavens, and see;
and behold the clouds, which are higher than you.

—*Job* 35:5

PATTERNS OF DELIGHT

Even with little else to see
Of the world's bewildering array
Of form and color, one might be
Well occupied, day after day,
Observing clouds. Enormous black
And silver clouds ballooning by,
And gray outrider clouds that crack
Explosive whips across the sky,
And chubby little puffs of white
And pink, and massive piles of gold—
So many patterns of delight,
So various, the sky can hold,
Our eyes would have enough to do
Without this earth to notice too!

FOR THE CHANGEFUL PANORAMA of the clouds we thank thee, Lord, and for the continuing fascination of seeing them alter in shape and color before our eyes. We thank thee for the shining castles of clouds that our childhood dreams inhabited on summer afternoons, and for the joy of entering them again sometimes in present days. We dreamed large dreams on summer afternoons when we were children, Lord; we had high aspirations and desires. Grant that we may keep in all our later living, in spite of disappointments and defeats, something of the hope and vision of our earliest sunlit days. In the name of Christ. AMEN.

> Thou hast granted me life and steadfast love;
> and thy care has preserved my spirit.
>
> —*Job* 10:12

ALWAYS WITH WONDER

Always with wonder I have looked at each
Recurring commonplace of every day:
At dawn skies deepening into luminous peach
And turquoise radiance, serenely gay;
At flash of wings across unclouded noons;
At trees stirred tranquilly by winds' caressing,
And fleecy clouds that nestle tiny moons,
And stars bestowing their eternal blessing.

These many days I've lived, perhaps I should
Take daily commonplaces quite for granted;
But it is God who granted them, these good
And lovely sights at which I gaze, enchanted,
Always with wonder widening my eyes,
Always with gratitude and glad surprise.

FATHER IN HEAVEN, may our hearts retain, through all our days, a glad responsiveness to loveliness wherever we may find it, whether in earth and sky or in human lives and spirits. Help us to keep through living's many changes the power of spontaneous delight in small familiar blessings, and a spirit of eager zest for new discoveries and undertakings. In Christ's name. AMEN.

With long life I will satisfy him,
and show him my salvation.

—Ps. 91:16

INDEPENDENCE

Her father is a sturdy man,
A silent man, who lives alone
With cats and dogs and memories
Of eighty Aprils he has known.

Each week she bakes a loaf of bread,
And two small spicy apple pies
And takes them to the silent man
With eighty Aprils in his eyes.

And this is all he lets her do,
The silent man whose eyes are keen
And apt to mirth, remembering
The eighty Aprils he has seen.

WE ARE GRATEFUL, O GOD, for the encouragement and inspiration of those who in the wisdom of long years are of a cheerful heart and optimistic spirit. May we reverence the richness of their experience and the ripeness of their judgment, and sincerely honor them for their overcoming of life's many trials. And may thy goodness and thy mercy never fail them, Lord; grant them secure dwellings and tender companions, and health of spirit, soul, and body all their days. In Christ's name. AMEN.

Let thy face shine on thy servant.—Ps. *31:16*

PHOTOGRAPH

The camera caught the clearness of her eyes,
And all their humorous kindness, which has caused
Us whom she most regards to realize
The worth of going on, when we had paused,
Uncertain of ourselves and of the way.
The camera caught the smiling confidence
With which she greets the least propitious day,
Calmly dispelling problems with good sense.

All this the camera caught, and scarcely could
Avoid, indeed, since all of this is so
Visibly present in her serenely good
Victorious face. But the picture does not show
How many faces are cheered, and luminous
With love, because of all she is to us.

WE THANK THEE, HEAVENLY FATHER, for faces expressing the
beauty of lives lived in the light of thy countenance. We con-
template with grateful and loving hearts the radiance reflected
in such faces, and remember the quiet and powerful influence
for good of such lives. We thank thee, Lord, that thou hast
lifted up the light of thy countenance upon them and given
them peace. In Christ's name. AMEN.

Those who trust in the Lord are like Mount Zion,
which cannot be moved, but abides for ever.

—*Ps. 125:1*

FARMER IN TOWN

He was a tall man standing there,
As tall as the hills that fathered him.
His shoulders were bent, the better to bear
The weight of the sky. His mouth was grim
With the strength of a thousand victories won
Over the wilds of wind and weather.
His eyes were kind as the equal sun
That blesses the evil and good together.

He stood in silence amid the throng
Of little men of the lesser air,
And seeing him standing, gaunt and long,
They went their way with a smiling stare—
Feeling a baffled, swift defeat
When a mountain stood in a city street.

WE THANK THEE, LORD OF THE EARTH, for those who till the
earth with faith and integrity. We thank thee for all who, toiling
steadfastly and with constant patience to bring forth the necessary treasures of the earth, bring forth as well good treasures from
their hearts, abiding magnanimity and kindness, a mountain
stature of good character. Grant us all to live by the essential
virtues, Lord, of sure fidelity and wise forbearance. In Christ's
name. AMEN.

106

Each dawn he does not fail.—*Zeph.* 3:5

RESPONSIBLE

She rose and looked at morning, what there was
Of it. A little line of deepening gold
Above the backyard roofs, she told herself,
Was as authentic gold as that which shone
Above the curving unencumbered hills
That rose from wide remembered meadowlands.
"I wonder if anybody's watching there.
I used to think dawn couldn't turn out well
Unless I saw it come. I know it does.
The menfolks, children, chickens, get
   their breakfasts,
And food gets canned. The things I did get done—
Or if they don't nobody misses them.
Not many think dawn needs their help these days.
But even if the folks are all asleep,
This golden light is shining on the hills,
And even here it gives the early clumps
Of smoke that grow upon the almost-clean
Dawn sky an edge of gold. Coal smoke
   from chimneys
Or mist on hills, it's much the same to dawn."
And though it wasn't much the same to her,
There were the books she'd always meant to read,
A letter to the woman overseas
To write, a dress to make for the child next door.
Much could be done with daylight, even here—
Too much for sleeping late. Whether it came
On misty hill or smoky backyard lawn
She'd always feel responsible for dawn.

We thank thee, lord, for all who co-operate with thee in
bringing light and gladness to the world. amen.

107

THE SONG BEYOND

It always seemed to her, her whole life through,
There was a song that only she could sing
Waiting a little way beyond the blue
Clear air of evening gentled by the wing
Of one white bird, a little way beyond
The haze that lay forever on her hills;
A song to which men's spirits must respond,
Forgetting, for a little, all their ills.

The song was always there, but when she tried
To voice its words and melody, it fell
Dull on her ears, and all the wonder died.
If it was bane or bliss, she could not tell,
To hear not far away, her whole life long,
Faint whispers of an uncreated song.

O GOD, thou knowest how far short of what we dreamed and hoped and planned our best endeavors always seem to fall. Always the perfect work eludes us, Lord; always our highest goal is unattained. Yet we are grateful for the constant aspiration, for the persistent hope, ever renewed and renewing, that each new work may more nearly fulfill our best ideal. Help us, Lord, always with hopeful hearts to give our best to whatever work we do; and when we are freed of earthly limitations, Father, may we serve thee perfectly. In Christ's name. AMEN.

The Lord is near to the broken-hearted,
and saves the crushed in spirit.

—*Ps. 34:18*

FIRST CHRISTMAS AFTER LOSS

"The Christmas star shines everywhere,"
  she thought.
"I know the Christmas star shines everywhere—
But can I spend this Christmas as I ought
In a strange land that he will never share?

"The Christmas star is bright in any land.
He is with God, beyond the star, I know.
But, Lord, I miss the warm touch of his hand,
I miss his smile, I miss him, miss him so."

When she arose that lonely Christmas day,
The eastern sky was warm with rosy light,
And in the tender loveliness the ray
Of one white star was shining, pure and bright.

She whispered, "Lord, how great thy mercies are
In showing me this day the Christmas star."

FATHER IN HEAVEN, in time of utmost sorrow may we humbly trust in thee. May thy goodness abide with us and comfort us, and thy mercy preserve our hearts in faith and hope. May we cast all our care upon thee, Lord, assured that thou wilt give us the help we need to live courageously, not darkening others' gladness by our grief. And teach our yearning hearts, O God, sincerely to rejoice that the one we love, released of earthly trials and limitations, has entered into fuller life with thee. In Christ's name. AMEN.

This is none other than the house of God, and this is the gate of heaven.—*Gen. 28:17*

NEVER A LAST GOOD-BY

Somehow my heart can never learn to say
A last good-by, entirely and completely,
To anything I ever loved. There may
Be folk who can accomplish severance neatly
With no loose ends of longing and regret
To trip their hearts at unexpected hours;
But always my heart stumbles, even yet,
When the shape of hills or the rain-sweet
   scent of flowers
Recalls my earliest home, or when the sound
Of laughter echoes that which used to fall
From lips long silent to me. I am bound
By myriad threads of memory, keeping all
I ever loved so near me still, that I
Shall never learn to say a last good-by.

WE THANK THEE, O GOD, that through the grace of Christ our Savior we need not say a last good-by to those we love. We thank thee for the promise of eternal life in him, and for faith that all we have ever known of goodness, truth, and beauty shall continue and shall be made perfect. O everlasting God, our faithful shepherd, whose goodness and mercy hath followed us all the days of our lives, we thank thee that in whatever of thy many mansions we may dwell, thy goodness and thy mercy shall follow us forever. In Christ's name. AMEN.

The Library of Congress has
cataloged this book as follows:

Merchant, Jane. In green pastures; [poems] New
   York, Abingdon Press [1959]. 110 p. 16 cm.
   1. Devotional exercises. i. Title. BV4832.2.M4
   242   59–8199 ‡